W9-DIJ-249

The

Jabez
You
Never
Knew

Hebraic Keys to Answered Prayers

THE JABEZ YOU NEVER KNEW

Hebraic Keys to Answered Prayers

©2013 Norm Franz
Second Edition

ISBN 0-971-0863-1-1

Published by Ascension Ministries

For information on the ministry of Norm Franz
Visit www.ascensionministries.net

All rights reserved. This book may not be copied or reprinted for commercial gain or profit of any kind. The use of short quotations or occasional copying for personal or group Bible study is permitted and encouraged. Brief quotations embodied in critical articles or reviews are also permitted.

Unless otherwise noted, all Scripture quotations and references are from the New American Standard Bible. ©The Lockman Foundation 1960, 1962, 1963, 1968, 1971, 1972, 1973, 1975, 1977

All emphasis of Scripture references by the author are in italics.

02 03 10 9 8 7 6 5 4 3 2 1

Cover design by Ivy Ho
Interior design by David Ong

TABLE OF CONTENTS

DEDICATION

THIS BOOK is dedicated to the millions of prayer warriors throughout the ages, who have interceded with God and waged a good warfare through prayer.

My hope and prayer is that it contributes to God's refining fire that is currently purging the end time prayer movement, and that it be found among the prayers of the saints which appear before God's throne at the end of the age (Revelation 5:8; 8:3).

In God's Love,
NORM FRANZ
A Messenger of the Covenant

INTRODUCTION

*"And Jabez was more honourable than his
brethren: and his mother called his name
Jabez, saying, because I bare him with sorrow.
And Jabez called on the God of Israel, saying,
Oh that thou wouldest bless me indeed, and
enlarge my coast, and that thine hand might be
with me, and that thou wouldest keep me from
evil, that it may not grieve me! And God granted him that which he requested."*
1 Chronicles 4:9-10, KJV

THE CURRENT WORLDWIDE prayer movement has become a spiritual phenomenon that
has mobilized the church like never before. It has
brought the intercessory prayers of the saints to bear
on the 10/40 window with tremendous results for the
glory of God. This intense global prayer plays a ma-
jor role in the end time events that mark the season of
the Lord's return (Revelation 5:8; 8:3-4).

However, with every movement there inevitably
comes the misapplication of biblical truth. Whether it
has come from an overzealous lack of knowledge or
an outright attempt at deception, the same thing has
happened within certain areas of the prayer move-

1

ment. Similarly, I believe much of the teaching surrounding the prayer of Jabez is one of those areas.

The prayer of Jabez has become a rave among many in the Christian community around the world. I first discovered this while on an extended ministry trip to Southeast Asia, where I heard Christians praying this prayer in semi-rote fashion.

I quickly learned that people were doing this because a growing number of international Christian leaders "guaranteed" that by praying this prayer three or four times a day God would be obligated to answer it just as He did for Jabez. Many even promised that the lives of the people who regularly prayed this prayer would be "marked by miracles," and that the timetable for these "guaranteed miracles" was generally around "30 days."[1]

Because of my Hebraic understanding of Scripture, I was horrified at this theology. Anyone who studies the Bible with even the smallest degree of Hebraic hermeneutics knows that any kind of rote prayer has never and will never work to produce God's blessing.

"Praying through" according to the will of God and the leading of the Holy Spirit is one thing, but repetitive prayer for the purpose of compelling God into doing something favorable on our behalf is not the way of Yahweh (YHVH).

Rote vs Righteous Prayer

This type of repetitive prayer to acquire something from God has its origins in ancient pagan religion that goes all the way back to Nimrod's Babylon. Today, this practice has evolved into an assortment of ritualistic prayers which use everything from "prayer wheels" to various types of beads for counting the number of times each prayer is repeated.

Abstaining from this form of pagan mantra is what Yeshua (Jesus) was referring to when He said:

> "And when you are praying, *do not use meaningless repetition*, as the Gentiles [heathens] do, for they suppose that they will be heard for their many words. Therefore *do not be like them*; for your Father knows what you need, before you ask Him." (Matthew 6:7-8)

In other words, God will not give us what we want just because we pray a certain prayer three or four or even 1,000 times in a day. When we do this, we are putting our trust in the prayer instead of God, and it becomes a form of idolatry.

From a Hebraic perspective, prayers recorded in the Bible were never intended to be repeated verbatim by successive generations as a way of getting

God to move. They were recorded to provide a historical record of how heartfelt, Spirit-led, obedience-driven prayer moves the heart of God.

They also supply us with an outline when formulating our own prayers. We know this is true because, immediately after telling us not to pray repetitious prayers, Yeshua gives us what seems to be a repetitious entreaty known as the "Lord's Prayer" (Matthew 6:9-13). This appears contradictory unless we understand that, in the Hebraic culture, the rabbis would often put forth *prayer outlines*. These outlines were simply reminders to include certain points within their prayers that were scripturally pleasing to God. This type of prayer outline is actually what many Bible scholars believe Yeshua gave us in the "Lord's Prayer."

In this light, I believe the prayer of Jabez can be used as the same type of prayer outline, but I don't believe God ever intended for it to be prayed verbatim in a repetitive fashion. That is because God only answers prayer that is from a Spirit-led heart of love and obedience to Him, which is exactly the way Jabez offered his prayer. Unfortunately, this pure and simple prayer has been turned into a religious chant for obtaining success that Yeshua said we should not emulate.

Praying Amiss

The biggest mistake people make in their life is that they "ask amiss." Their lack of knowledge concerning God's ways allows them to fall into the trap of believing that their own agenda and lustful desires are the will of God. This causes them to pray after those lusts and consequently their prayers go unanswered:

> "Ye ask, and receive not, because ye ask amiss, that ye may consume it upon your lusts." (James 4:3, KJV)

They do not know God's will because they have never allowed Him to write His laws (Torah[2]) upon their hearts, which is the primary way He makes Himself and His will known to us (Jeremiah 31:31-34; Psalms 40:8). Seeking after their own desires instead of God's indicates their hearts are filled with a measure of iniquity, in which case the Lord will not hear their prayer:

> "If I regard iniquity in my heart, the Lord will not hear me." (Psalm 66:18, KJV)

Whenever Israel asked for God's blessing while simultaneously walking in disobedience, Scripture teaches that God became "angry" with their prayers

(Psalm 80:4). They were going through all the ceremony and programmed ritual of playing church, but they were walking in sin (Isaiah 1:10-15). They even fell into the same pagan trap of offering repetitious prayer like many in the church today. Whenever this happens, God hides Himself and refuses to hear our prayers:

> "So when you spread out your hands in prayer, *I will hide my eyes from you*; yes, even though you *multiply* [repeat] *prayers, I will not listen.*" (Isaiah 1:15)

Solomon also makes it clear that, if we refuse to obey God's Torah, He views our prayers in a very negative light:

> "He who turns away his ear from listening to the law [*Torah*], even his prayer is an abomination." (Proverbs 28:9)

Purpose of this Book

The purpose of this book is not to discredit the prayer of Jabez, but to help the body of Messiah Yeshua understand that God does not answer prayers just because we pray. He answers prayers that are in line with His will and come from a heart of love for

God. This love always results in obedience to His word, which leads us to walk upright and righteous before Him. Under these circumstances, God not only hears our prayers, but He delights in them:

> "The sacrifice of the wicked is an abomination to the Lord, but the prayer of the upright is His delight...The Lord is far from the wicked, but He hears the prayer of the righteous." (Proverbs 15:8, 29)

In this light, we will see that the prayer of Jabez is not about the prayer itself, but an honorable man named Jabez and his relationship with Yahweh God. This makes Jabez the perfect study for establishing the real reason why God "granted him that which he requested."

ONE

WHO WAS JABEZ?

"Jabez was more honourable than his brethren"

IN ANCIENT ISRAEL, children were generally given their names eight days after they were born, when they were presented for dedication in the temple or synagogue. The boys were also circumcised at this time, and their names were declared publicly. The reason for the delay in naming the children was because whatever primary characteristic they displayed during those eight days generally served as the foundation of their name.

Jabez (Hebrew: "Ya'beets") means "he causes pain," which undoubtedly marked the critical circumstances in which his mother bore him – i.e., she "bore him with pain". Most theologians believe this is referring to a long difficult labor or maybe even something as severe as breech delivery. Whatever the case, she named him Jabez (Septuagint: "Igabees"), because his most memorable characteristic, from his mother's point of view, was that he caused her immense pain that first day.

Doctor of the Torah

Jewish writers and ancient historians affirm that Jabez grew up to become an eminent doctor in the law.[3] In fact, his reputation for piety and insight into God's Torah drew so many scribes around him that a town was named after him[4] (1 Chronicles 2:55).

To be a sought-after instructor of God's Torah was a very coveted position. One in which his mother must have found recompense for all her trials at delivery. It was also an obvious testimony of how God can take our pain and turn it into a blessing.

Jabez not only understood the true purpose of God's Torah, but he obviously walked in those truths. This produced faithfulness to God that is eulogized in the opening passage "and Jabez was more honorable than his brothers".

But what was it that made Jabez more honorable than his brothers? Was this eulogy bestowed him based on man's standard of honorability or was it God's standard? Why of course, it was God's standard as defined in Scripture. This is where God's Torah, as ministered by His servants the prophets, cannot be denied.

I want to submit that it was his high level of holy commitment to God's Laws (Torah) that earned him the noble distinction of being "more honorable than his brothers." This point is more obvious in the Chaldee version of this Scripture passage, because it links his honor directly to his expertise in the law[5]:

> "And Jabets also, he is Othniel, *honourable and skilled in the law beyond his brethren*, whose mother called his name Jabets, because she had borne him in sorrow."
> (1 Chronicles 4:9, CV)

Here we see that his high degree of honor was directly connected to his advanced knowledge of the Torah. This does not mean that his brothers were not honorable or untaught in God's word. It just means that Jabez was more honorable because of his high degree of understanding and commitment to it. This is an eternal truth that is based on how a man conducts himself in relation to God's ways as expressed in the Scriptures.

Humility and the Fear of the Lord

Many of God's ways are expressed in the writings of King Solomon, which the Lord uses to establish His standards for who qualifies as an honorable man:

"The fear of the LORD is the instruction of wisdom; and before *honour* is humility." (Proverbs 15:33, KJV)

"By humility and the fear of the LORD are riches, and *honour*, and life." (Proverbs 22:4, KJV)

Here, we see that an honorable man has a holy fear of the Lord, which leads him to walk humbly before Yahweh God. Consequently, these two characteristics had to be evident in Jabez' life in order for him to qualify as an honorable man.

The question is; do we, who pray this prayer today, have the same fear of the Lord that Jabez had? An even more important question is; do we even know what the fear of the Lord really is? King Solomon gives us a clear definition when he says:

"The fear of the LORD is to hate evil: pride, and arrogancy, and the evil way, and the froward mouth, do I hate." (Proverbs 8:13, KJV)

Here, it is easy to surmise that evil is referring to sin, which the apostle John defines as "the transgression of the Law [Torah]" (1 John 3:4, KJV). Therefore, a man who truly fears the Lord has a hatred of sin that results in his obedience to God's commandments:

"And the LORD commanded us to *do all these statutes*, to *fear the LORD our God*, for our good always, that he might preserve us alive, as it is this day." (Deuteronomy 6:24, KJV)

Please note that obedience is not for salvation, but "for our good always, that [God] might preserve us alive." This is especially true in the New Covenant, because these same laws are supposed to be written on our hearts that we might come to know and obey God (Jeremiah 31:31-34).

Since the "wages of sin (breaking God's Laws) is death," the *fear of the Lord* is also man's dread of the penalty for breaking those Laws. It was the *fear of the Lord* that came on the early church when Ananias and Sapphira suffered the penalty of physical death for breaking the ninth commandment not to lie (Acts 5:11). As the church matured, those who walked in the *fear of the Lord* (obedience to God's commandments) enjoyed the peace of God and were comforted by the Holy Spirit (Acts 9:31).

This simply means that Jabez had a *fear of the Lord* that caused him to walk in humble obedience to God's laws, therefore qualifying him as an honorable man.

Righteousness Brings Honor

Solomon also said that God honors those who choose to live a righteous life:

> "*He who pursues righteousness* and loyalty finds life, righteousness and *honor*."
> (Proverbs 21:21)

Every believer wants to pursue God's righteousness, but most have never been taught what God's righteousness is, or what it is supposed to look like. For most Christians, righteousness is just a positive confession that never fully manifests in their lives. In other words, there is a lot of talk without much action.

Solomon learned what righteousness was from his father David, who said:

> "My tongue shall speak of thy word: *for all thy commandments are righteousness*."
> (Psalm 119:172, KJV)

David obviously learned this truth as he meditated on God's law (Psalm 1:1-2), which is holy and *righteous* and good (Romans 7:12). The foundation of this truth comes from the Torah as given by Moses:

"And it shall be our righteousness, *if we observe to do all these commandments* before the LORD our God, as he hath commanded us." (Deuteronomy 6:25, KJV)

Righteousness is received by faith, strengthened in confession, and perfected through obedience. In other words, a righteous man is one who pursues the manifestation of God's righteousness in his life through his obedience to the Word. This is known in both the Old and New Testaments as the "practice of righteousness," which is what the apostle John was referring to when he said:

"Little children, let no one deceive you; *the one who practices righteousness is righteous*, just as He is righteous." (1 John 3:7)

Again, it is important to clarify that we are saved and become the righteousness of God by grace through faith in His sacrifice on the cross (Ephesians 2:8-9). However, once this takes place, God's commandments instruct us how to practice (walk out) His righteousness in our lives.

Consequently, when a person walks in obedience to God's commandments, the Lord considers them to be "righteous as He is righteous" and He promises to answer their prayers:

"The effectual fervent prayer of a *righteous man* availeth much." (James 5:16b KJV)

"*For the eyes of the Lord are upon the righteous, and His ears attend to their prayer*, but the face of the Lord is against those who do evil." (1 Peter 3:12)

This means that Jabez, like Paul, pursued God's righteousness by being a doer of the Torah and not just a hearer (Romans 2:11-13). As a result, God's righteousness manifested in his life, and the Lord deemed him an *honorable* man.

Obedience Brings Honor

There are numerous biblical expressions that are used as synonyms for obedience. Terminology such as "serve God", "follow God", "listen to His voice", and "listen to His law" can all be translated as "obey God's commandments" or "follow God's ways" (Deuteronomy 30:17; Joshua 24:24; Daniel 7:27)

As we serve, follow, and listen to the Lord through the observance of His commandments, He honors us. This is what Yeshua meant when He said:

"If anyone *serves* [obeys] Me, let him *follow*

Me [My ways]; and where I am, there shall
My servant also be; if anyone *serves* [obeys]
Me, the Father will *honor* him." (John 12:26)

As an honorable man, this further confirms that
Jabez was walking in submission to God's commandments as given in the Torah. There is nowhere
in Scripture where God has ever *honored* anyone
who walked in willful disobedience to His Laws.
God loves everyone, even believers who are walking
in sin, but He only *honors* those who walk in obedience.

When referring to end time judgment, Paul asserts
that obedience conveys *honor* at Messiah's coming:
"But because of your stubbornness and unrepentant
heart you are storing up wrath for yourself in the day
of wrath and revelation of the righteous judgment of
God, who will *render to every man according to his
deeds: to those who by perseverance in doing good*
seek for glory and *honor* and immortality, eternal
life; but to those who are selfishly ambitious and do
not obey the truth, but obey unrighteousness [*dis-
obey God's commandments*], wrath and indignation."
(Romans 2:5-8)

It is important to note that Paul is talking to the
born again believers in the church at Rome, who

were predominately gentiles in the flesh. He is telling them that *honor* is given by God based on their good deeds, which he further defines as obedience to the Torah (verses 11-14). Paul makes it abundantly clear that when we obey the truth it brings us honor. Whereas, those who are selfish, ambitious and "do not obey the truth" receive wrath and indignation.

What is the Truth?

When asked "what is the truth", most of God's people proudly assert that "Yeshua is the truth," which is correct. But what was the truth before Yeshua came?

Throughout the Scriptures, God declares that His word is His truth, and His truth is His word:

> "Thy righteousness is an everlasting righteousness, and *Thy law* [Torah] *is truth.*" (Psalm 119:142)

> "Thou art near, O Lord, and *all Thy commandments are truth.*" (Psalm 119:151)

> "*The sum of Thy word is truth,* and every one of Thy righteous ordinances is everlasting." (Psalm 119:160)

David is saying that the essence (life) of God is truth, which He has revealed to us in His word. Consequently, when Yeshua referred to Himself as "the *way*, and the *truth*, and the *life*" (John 14:6), He was saying that He was the very *life* of Yahweh God, who was the Word become flesh to show us the *way* of *truth* (John 1:1-4,14).

To Know the Truth

Yeshua also taught that, if we wanted to "know the *truth*" that sets us free, we have to "abide" in His word[6] (John 8:31-32; John 15:9-10; 1 John 2:24-28; Psalm 91:1). "Abide" comes from the Greek word "meno," which means: "to dwell, to live, *to remain as one*, not to leave, *to maintain unbroken fellowship*."[7]

A derivative of this word that is often used is "enmenoo", which summons God's servants to walk "in faithful obedience" to His commandments in order that they might live.[8]

In other words, Yeshua is saying that if we live in unbroken fellowship with His word, we become one with Him who is the truth. This is what is known as "living the Word."

This teaching was based on Yeshua' understanding of the Hebrew root word "yashab," which means: "to dwell, to settle, to cause (cities) to be inhabited, to *marry* (that is, to give an dwelling to), *to be inhabited.*" [9]

In other words, when we abide in the truth of God's word, we are married to Him and we become a dwelling place for His habitation. When we walk this out in our lives, it releases the New Jerusalem to be built in us, and sin (the transgression of God's Law) no longer has any place in us.

The Righteous Walk

This walk is identified in biblical terms as "the way" (Genesis 18:19; Exodus 18:20; Psalm 25:8; Mark 10:52; Acts 18:25-26), which is also referred to in Hebrew as "halacha" or "the righteous walk." This walk is empowered by the "Spirit of *truth*" who has come to "lead [us] in all the *truth*" (John 16:7-15). Hence, to really know the truth one must "abide" in it by walking obedient to God's word. As we do, His laws (truths) are written on our hearts, and we come to truly know Him, "for all will know him" (Jeremiah 31:31-34).

This means that Jabez was a man of faith who walked in righteous obedience to the truth of God's

Torah. This opened up the knowledge of God to him, and the more Jabez came to know the Lord the more he came to love Him. And the more he came to love Him, the more he obeyed Him (Exodus 20:6; John 14:15; 1 John 2:3-5). And the more he obeyed Him, the more he came to know Him, and so the cycle goes. This is how the Holy Spirit of God changed us from glory to glory into the image of Yeshua (2 Corinthians 3:18; Romans 8:29).

This process produced a humility and reverential fear of the Lord that made Jabez more honorable that his brothers. This is who Jabez was and why God "granted him that which he requested" (KJV).

TWO

BLESS ME LORD

"Oh that Thou wouldst bless me…"

THE FIRST THING that Jabez prayed for was that God would "bless" him. Some teach that the blessing of the Lord is synonymous with miracles that become commonplace in our lives, but this is not Scriptural. Miracles are an extension of God's grace and mercy to those who are in desperate need of supernatural deliverance.

On the other hand, the blessing of the Lord is when the spiritual, mental, and physical well-being of God is consistently being manifest in one's life because of their commitment to God. This is the *manifest blessing* of God that makes rich and adds no sorrow (Proverbs 10:22). Although miracles are a blessing when they come, a person who is in constant need of a miracle is most likely living under a curse.

Many times, those who crave miracles have impure motives, which Yeshua pointed out when He said, "An evil and adulterous generation seeks after a sign [miracle]" (Matthew 16:4). There's nothing wrong with miracles, but if we are seeking miracles first, and His Kingdom and His righteousness second, then we are in effect seeking another god.

To be blessed of the Lord is a godly desire that is in the heart of all His people, and Jabez was no different. However, as a Torah observant Jew, Jabez understood that all the desire and prayer in the world would not produce God's blessing in his life, because God's blessing comes differently.

Love Produces God's Blessing

Through the prophet Moses, God gives clear and unambiguous instructions on what produces His blessing in a person's life:

> "See, I have set before you today life and prosperity, and death and adversity; in that I command you today to *love the LORD your God, to walk in His ways and to keep His commandments and His statutes and His judgments*, that you may live and multiply, and that the LORD your God may *bless you* in the land where you are entering to possess it." (Deuteronomy 30:15-16)

The first and foremost commandment is to "love the Lord your God with all your heart, with all your soul, and with all your strength" (Deuteronomy 6:5; Mark 12:30). This love comes as the natural and immediate response to God's love for us and the salvation He has given us in Messiah Yeshua. This is a tangible supernatural experience, where God's love is shed abroad in our hearts by His Spirit, which then enables us to love Him (Romans 5:5; 1 John 4:19).

Yet, in the above passage of Scripture, Moses goes on to indicate that our love for God will lead us "to walk in His ways and to keep His commandments and His statutes and His judgments." It must be understood that this truth did not pass away when Yeshua came. Yeshua Himself came as a prophet like Moses (Acts 3:22) and confirmed this truth when He said:

> "If you love Me, you will keep My commandments." (John 14:15)

Consequently, as we love God and obey His commandments, He *blesses* us according to the promise He made in the Torah. This is part of what Paul meant when he said, "we know that the Law is good, if one uses it lawfully" (1 Timothy 1:8). However, if we use the Law in order to get saved, to get righteous, or even to get blessed, it is an unlawful use of the Law. Moreover this misuse comes from a works-righteousness mentality that is actually anti-Torah.

Hence, we obey God's Laws because we love Him, and because it reflects His very nature and character that He is working to fulfill in us (Romans 8:3-4). Out of that love, flows a pure and holy obedience to God's word that produces more blessings than we can handle:

> "Now it shall be, *if you will diligently obey the LORD your God, being careful to do all His commandments* which I command you today, the LORD your God will set you high above all the nations of the earth. And *all these blessings shall come upon you and overtake you, if you will obey the LORD your God*." (Deuteronomy 28:1-2)

Simply put, God's *manifest blessing* comes as a result of a person's love-based obedience to His commandments. This type of obedience moves God to "command" His blessing in every area of our lives:

> "The LORD will *command the blessing upon you* in your barns and in all that you put your hand to, and He will *bless you* in the land which the LORD your God gives you... And the LORD shall make you the head and not the tail, and you only shall be above, and you

shall not be underneath, *if you will listen to the commandments of the LORD your God*, which I charge you today, *to observe them carefully...*" (Deuteronomy 28:8, 13)

Many of God's people like to pray and confess that they are "the head and not the tail" and "above and not beneath," but then they refuse to "listen to the commandments of the LORD" and "observe them carefully," which is the qualifier. As a result, many wonder why they are not blessed. Others simply live in dysfunctional denial, where they continually confess that they are blessed when, in fact, they are living under the curse of disobedience without realizing it.

Blessings and Cursings

The principle of blessing and cursing goes all the way back to the Garden of Eden. It is known as the "law of sin and death," where Adam's sin (breaking God's Law) released the curse of death upon the whole earth. Since then, the law of blessings for obedience and cursings for disobedience has been in the earth.

This was even true in the life of Abraham and Sarah when they disobeyed God's word that said they were going to have a child together. Their disobedience came when they allowed Hagar to wed and conceive Ishmael with Abraham. Their disobedience produced the curse of Ishmael that is at the heart of today's Middle East conflict (Genesis 16:11-12).

Once they got past that detour and had their son Isaac, God tested Abraham's faith by *commanding* him to sacrifice Isaac. While Abraham was in the middle of obeying that commandment, Yahweh not only provided a sacrificial ram as a substitute for Isaac, but He released His blessing on Abraham and his descendants in the form of a ratified oath:

> "Then the angel of the LORD called to Abraham a second time from heaven, and said, '*By Myself I have sworn*, declares the LORD, *because you have done this thing* [obeyed Me], *and have not withheld your son*, your only son, indeed I will *greatly bless you*, and I will greatly multiply your seed as the stars of the heavens, and as the sand which is on the seashore; and your seed shall possess the gate of their enemies.'" (Genesis 22:15-17)

The Promise of Abraham

It is important to understand that Abraham's election was unconditional according to God's sovereign will. Equally important is that Yahweh's promise to Abraham was based on Abraham's righteousness that was by faith. However, his faith was perfected through his works of obedience to God's commandment, which is what proved his righteousness and qualified him to receive the blessing (James 2:17-24).

God reaffirms this equation when He passed the promise of Abraham on to Isaac and his descendants. Please note that this reaffirmation was not just because Abraham was willing to offer up Isaac, but because he was obedient to God's Torah as a whole:

> "Sojourn in this land and I will be with you and *bless you*, for to you and to your descendants I will give all these lands, and *I will establish the oath* which I swore to your father Abraham. And I will multiply your descendants as the stars of heaven, and will give your descendants all these lands; and by your descendants all the nations of the earth shall be *blessed; because Abraham obeyed Me and kept My charge, My commandments, My statutes, and My laws* [Torah]." (Genesis 26:3-5)

This is the unchanging law of sowing and reaping that is clearly carried forward into the New Covenant

(Genesis 2:17; Jeremiah 2:17-19, 4:18; John 5:14; Galatians 6:7-9).

New Covenant Seed of Abraham

In the New Covenant, believers are all one in Messiah Yeshua and subject to the same conditions of the Abrahamic promise:

> "There is neither Jew nor Greek, there is neither bond nor free, there is neither male nor female: for ye are all one in Christ Jesus. And if you be Christ's, then are ye Abraham's seed, and *heirs according to the promise.*" (Galatians 3:28-29, KJV)

It's important to remember that Yeshua is Yahweh incarnate, and He does not change. Therefore, His commandments in the New Testament are no different from the ones He gave in the Old Testament (John 15:10; Matthew 16:16-19). The difference is that in the New Covenant God writes them on our hearts and them baptizes us with His Spirit which empowers us to keep them. Consequently, in the New Covenant, God's blessings still come through obedience.

Throughout the history of God's relationship with

30

His people, He has never blessed our disobedience. He has tolerated it and kept us alive hoping that we would repent. He has even held back much of the punishment that is due because of it, but *He has never blessed it*. And in the end, everyone will reap what they sow regardless of how many times they pray the prayer of Jabez.

Jabez understood the truth and because he obeyed God from a heart of love, he could pray this prayer with confidence, knowing that God would answer it. Please note that Jabez did not pray his prayer three or four times a day, every day, hoping God would somehow be coerced into blessing him. It appears that he prayed it only once, which simply released the blessing that he was entitled to according to the covenant that God made with the fathers Abraham, Isaac and Jacob. And that same promise is ours today.

THREE

ENLARGE MY BORDERS LORD

"... and enlarge my coast [borders]..."

T HE NEXT THING Jabez prayed for was that God would enlarge his coast referring to his borders or boundaries. Many commentators believe that part of Jabez' prayer had to do with the conquest of the Promised Land, which was the heart of God's plan for expanding Israel's borders.

This is important to note, because Jabez wasn't asking God to expand his borders just because he wanted more land, but because expanding Israel's borders was part of God's specific will. Today, many Christians pray that God would expand their borders simply because they want more. They don't have a real purpose for it; they just want more to satisfy their fleshly pleasures:

> "You ask and do not receive, because you ask with wrong motives, so that you may spend it on your pleasures." (James 4:3)

In fact, during the financial boom of the 1990s, God showed me that many of His people had accumulated more money than they had vision for God. As a result, they spent their money, along with borrowed money, expanding their borders in the form of bigger homes, bigger cars, bigger boats, etc. In other words, they fed the lusts of their flesh rather than establishing God's covenant, which is why He prospers us in the first place (Deuteronomy 8:18).

Today, many are reaping this iniquity in the form of financial slavery to the debt system, failed businesses, bankruptcy, broken marriages and the destruction of families. Their lack of knowledge and obedience to God's ways has actually caused their boundaries to shrink.

Obedience Enlarges Boundaries

On the other hand, through his knowledge of the Torah, Jabez understood that expanding one's boundaries was simply part of God's blessing to those who walked obedient to His covenant. This promise was made to the fathers Abraham, Isaac, and Jacob and extended to the children of Israel when they came out of Egypt on their way to the Promised Land:

> "Hear, O Israel! The LORD is our God, the LORD is one! And *you shall love the LORD your God with all your heart and with all*

your soul and with all your might. And these words, which I am commanding you today, *shall be on your heart*; and you shall teach them diligently to your sons and shall talk of them when you sit in your house and when you walk by the way and when you lie down and when you rise up... Then it shall come about *when the LORD your God brings you into the land [expands your borders]* which He swore to your fathers, Abraham, Isaac and Jacob, to give you, great and splendid cities which you did not build, and houses full of all good things which you did not fill, and hewn cisterns which you did not dig, vineyards and olive trees which you did not plant, and you shall eat and be satisfied..." (Deuteronomy 6:4-7, 10-11)

This unbelievable blessing of expanded borders was promised to Israel in return for their love-based obedience to God's commandments. Yahweh reaffirms this expansion of borders by giving the children of Israel a promise within The Promise:

"Wherefore I command thee, saying, Thou shalt separate three cities for thee. And if the LORD thy God *enlarge thy coast* [borders], as he hath sworn unto thy fathers, and give thee all the land which he promised to give unto thy fathers; *if thou shalt keep all these commandments to do them*, which I command thee this day, *to love the LORD thy God, and to walk ever in his ways; then shalt thou add three cities more for thee* [enlarge your borders], beside these three..." (Deuteronomy 19:7-9, KJV; also see Deuteronomy 15:4-6)

Here, we see that God will enlarge our borders *if* we purpose to keep all His commandments, to love Him, and to walk ever in His ways. If we are unwilling to follow this eternal model, we cannot expect Him to increase our boundaries just because we pray the prayer of Jabez. This would put prayer above God's word, and not even His own name is above His word (Psalm 138:2).

What Commandments Do We Obey?

Right now, many of you are asking; what commandments do we need to obey in order for God to enlarge our boundaries? That's a good question. I am so glad you asked, because God's word gives us some specific direction concerning this matter.

Obviously, we need to obey the Ten Commandments, because they are the very foundation of God's covenant:

> "So He declared to you *His covenant* which He commanded you to perform, that is, the *Ten Commandments*; and He wrote them on two tablets of stone." (Deuteronomy 4:13)

However, there are other commandments, statutes, and ordinances that will expand our borders if we observe them:

> "You shall work six days, but on the seventh day you shall rest; even during plowing time and harvest you shall rest. And you shall celebrate the Feast of Weeks [*Pentecost*], that is, the first fruits of the wheat harvest, and the Feast of Ingathering [*Sukkot – Feast of Tabernacles*] at the turn of the year. Three times a year all your males are to appear before the Lord GOD, the God of Israel. For I will drive out nations before you and *enlarge your borders*, and no man shall covet your land when you go up three times a year to appear before the LORD your God." (Exodus 34:21-24)

Here we see that the Lord directly connects enlarging our borders together with our willingness to keep His appointed times/feasts (Leviticus 23). He begins with His appointed Sabbath, which starts at sundown Friday and ends at sundown on Saturday. This time is very important to God and to us, because it is one of the truths that His entire creation is built upon (Genesis 2:2-3).

God also includes His Sabbath as the fourth commandment of His covenant, which He establishes as a sign between Him and His people:

> "And the LORD spoke to Moses, saying, 'But as for you, speak to the sons of Israel, saying, 'You shall surely observe My Sabbaths; for this is a sign between Me and you throughout your generations, that you may know that I am the LORD who sanctifies you.'"'' (Exodus 31:12-13)

Some of you might be saying that this was the Old Covenant and it does not pertain to New Covenant believers. If you hold to that flawed theology, just remember that the prayer of Jabez also comes from the Old Covenant, and therefore would not pertain to us either. Like it or not, you cannot have it both ways.

Notice that the Lord says we "shall celebrate the Feast of Pentecost" if we expect to have our boundaries enlarged. Keeping the feast of Pentecost is not about legalistic bondage to a ritual; it is about celebrating the blessing of Lord. The first time Israel experienced Pentecost was at Mt Sinai when God gave them His Ten Commandments. Then He took Moses to the top of the mountain and gave him the rest of the commandments that instruct us how to apply the Ten Commandments to every area of our life and relationship with others.

The first time the New Testament church observed Pentecost, they received the promise of the Father, which is the baptism of the Holy Spirit (Acts 1:1-8). This baptism endues us with power so that we can walk in obedience to God's commandments. However, if we are without knowledge of what this is really for, we think that "speaking in tongues" is what it's all about. As a result, we walk around praying in tongues all day thinking we are spiritual, when the truth is we are just religious. Although we need to pray in the Spirit (tongues) as a regular part of our life, a truly spiritual person is not one who just prays, but one who prays and obeys.

Can you imagine what would have happened if the disciples had disobeyed Yeshua' command to remain in Jerusalem until He sent forth this promise (Luke 24:49)? The thought of not staying in Jerusalem for Pentecost, because they were now "under grace," never entered their minds. Nor did it enter Paul's mind not to continue celebrating this feast years later when he is seen hurrying back to Jerusalem to keep Pentecost according to the Torah (Acts 20:16).

The Lord also cites the three feasts that all men over 20 years old are required to go up to Jerusalem to celebrate each year[10] (Deuteronomy 16:16-17). Pentecost is one of them, and the other two are Passover in the spring and the Feast of Tabernacles in the fall. This is just a small sampling of God's laws that we are commanded to follow, if we want God *to enlarge our borders*.

Unbelief and Disobedience
Revoke the Blessing

Unfortunately, Israel walked in unbelief. This means they lacked the faith it took to keep God's covenant (Ten Commandments). As a result of their disobedience to the covenant, the blessing was withheld and they could not enter into the promise. In other words, their boundaries were not enlarged, and they wandered 40 years in the wilderness until the next generation was old enough to go in and take the land God's way (Hebrews 3:16-19).

As Joshua led that generation up to take the land of Canaan, God reestablished the promise that He

40

made with their fathers Abraham, Isaac, and Jacob. Once more, God's promise was conditional on their compliance to His Torah:

> "Be strong and courageous, for you shall give this people possession of the land [*enlarge their borders*] which I swore to their fathers to give them. Only be strong and very courageous; *be careful to do according to all the law which Moses My servant commanded you;* do not turn from it to the right or to the left, so *that you may have success wherever you go*. This book of the law shall not depart from your mouth, but you shall meditate on it day and night, so that you may *be careful to do according to all that is written in it*; for then you will make your way prosperous, and then you will have success [*be blessed*]."
> (Joshua 1:6-8)

At first, the children of Israel kept God's covenant, and He blessed them on every side by fulfilling all the promises that He made to their fathers (Joshua 21:43-45). Unfortunately, they later abandoned God's Torah to walk in the sin of their own ways. Consequently, when they obeyed God, His blessing was poured out upon them and their boundaries were expanded. However, when they disobeyed, His blessing was withdrawn and their boundaries were cut back (Nehemiah 9:24-38).

Extending Our Boundaries

This truth is as valid for us today as it was for Jabez and the children of Israel. Specifically for us today, the Lord's commandment to bless Israel plays a vital role if we want to come into the fullness of our God-ordained boundaries:

> "When the Most High gave the nations their inheritance, when He separated the sons of man, He set the boundaries of the peoples according to the number of the sons of Israel." (Deuteronomy 32:8)

God is saying that as we actively support the increase in the number of the sons of Israel to their full measure, He will enlarge our boundaries to their full measure. However, whoever comes against Israel to decrease their numbers or interfere with their right to the Promised Land will reap destruction and see their boundaries dwindle. Such is the way of God no matter how many times we pray the prayer of Jabez.

Therefore, if we really want God to bless us and

expand our borders, we must not only walk in obedience to His *whole word*, but we must also add the *prayer of David* to our prayer list:

> "*Pray for the peace of Jerusalem*: May they prosper who love you. May peace be within your walls, and prosperity within your palaces. For the sake of my brothers and my friends, I will now say, 'May peace be within you.' For the sake of the house of the LORD our God [*the church*] I will seek your good." (Psalm 122:6-9)

FOUR

BE WITH ME LORD

"And that Thy hand might be with me…"

T HE NEXT THING that Jabez prayed for was that God's hand would be with him. This is a Hebrew phrase that centers on the word "hand" (Hebrew: "yad"). Having God's hand "with" or "on" us is highly desirable, because it signifies that God Himself has joined us in a common cause[11] (Exodus 23:1)

To be more specific, it does not mean that He has joined our cause, but that we have joined His cause. In doing so, we gain the benefit of His power to uphold His rule in our lives as we carry out His plans and purposes.

The Power of His Hand

God's "hand" is another term for God's "power" (Jeremiah 16:21), which Yeshua refers to as the "right hand of power" (Mark 14:62). The Hebrew language portrays the power of His hand upholding His authority like the "arm rest" of a throne supports a king.[12] As we are seated on that throne with Him, the power of His hand upholds and strengthens us by driving away fear and anxiousness (Isaiah 41:10).

Another illustration shows God placing His hand over the mouth of a cave. This is a figure of speech (anthropomorphism), by which God promises His protection (Exodus 33:21-23; Isaiah 49:2). When His hand is on us, we can run wherever He leads with supernatural endurance (1 Kings 18:46), and the Kingdom of God expands as the lost are saved (Acts 11:21).

Torah also teaches that the power of God's hand "does not wax short," which means that His word will come to pass in our lives, so we need to obey it (Numbers 11:23). Those who "know the hand of the Lord" also know the fear of the Lord (Joshua 4:24), and God promises to bless them with life, health, prosperity, and success (Joshua 1:5-7).

God Was With Solomon

God promised Solomon that, if he walked in all the ways of His Torah, He would be with him and build him a house like He did David:

> "Then it will be, that if you listen to all that I command you and walk in My ways, and do

46

what is right in My sight by observing My statutes and My commandments, as My servant David did, then I will be with you and build you an enduring house as I built for David, and I will give Israel to you." (1 Kings 11:38)

Scripture verifies that as long as Solomon walked in compliance to God's commandments, God blessed and built up Israel as a kingdom. But when he turned away from God, God's hand was no longer with him to establish the kingdom.

This does not mean that God did not love Solomon or that He would not forgive him if he repented. It means that when Solomon walked away from God's way of building the kingdom, he started to build his own kingdom and God was not with him to do this.

God's Hand is Heavy on Sin

At the same time God's hand was there to bless Israel's obedience; it was "heavy" on their enemies to smite them:

"Now the hand of the LORD was heavy on the Ashdodites, and He ravaged them and

47

smote them with tumors, both Ashdod and its territories." (1 Samuel 5:6)

However, when Israel fell into sin, God's hand had the opposite effect. Instead of it being heavy on their enemies, it was heavy on them and their enemies had power over them (2 Chronicles 28:5).

This is also true on an individual level, as when Job found himself in rebellion and under the hand of God:

> "Even today my complaint is rebellion; His hand is heavy despite my groaning." (Job 23:2)

Another example is when David walked in unrepentant transgression of the Torah; God's hand was heavy on him to the point where he lost his strength:

> "When I kept silent about my sin, my body wasted away through my groaning all day long. For day and night Your hand was heavy upon me; my vitality was drained away as with the fever heat of summer."
> (Psalm 32:3-4)

God's hand is not actually heavy on the individual; it is heavy on sin. Hence, when a person is in sin, it feels like God's hand is heavy on him. This is nothing more than sowing and reaping. God's hand is there to bless when we are obedient and absent when we are disobedient no matter how many times we pray the prayer of Jabez.

Is God's Hand Blessing You?

Today, many in the body of Christ mistakenly believe that by praying for God's hand to be on them it automatically produces a blessing. However, if they are walking in sin – known or unknown – God's hand goes against what they are doing.

When Yeshua promised never to leave us or forsake us, it was conditional on our obedience to His word. As long as we are discipling the nations by "teaching them to observe all that (Yeshua) commanded," He will never leave or forsake us because we are building His Kingdom His way (Matthew 28:19-20). However, the minute we start doing it any other way, we are building our own kingdom and He will not be with us to do that.

In the areas we are walking in accordance to His ways, He is with us establishing His Kingdom in our lives. However, in the areas that we are not doing it His way, He is not with us. This is one reason why so many of God's people live roller coaster lives. They are obeying in some areas and being blessed, but completely missing it in others and the blessing is withheld. They are consistently inconsistent, because they have never learned the ways of God according to His Torah.

Therefore, Jabez' commitment to walk in accordance with God's laws was the key to the Lord's hand being with him. In the same manner, as we study God's Torah and walk according to it, God's hand will also be with us.

FIVE

KEEP ME FROM EVIL LORD

"...that thou wouldest keep me from evil, that it may not grieve me!"

THE LAST REQUEST Jabez made was for God to keep him from evil, so that it would not grieve or pain him.[13]

He was not referring to the evil that someone might do to him that would grieve him, but the evil he might do that would bring grief back on him as a result:

> "Like watchmen of a field they are against her round about, because she has rebelled against Me," declares the LORD. "Your ways and your deeds have brought these things to you. This is your evil. How bitter! How it has touched your heart!" (Jeremiah 4:17-18)

The Way of Pain

Jabez understood that evil is sin, and its wages always bring pain, grief, and death back upon the sinner. In fact, the one common thesis that runs throughout the Scriptures is that all men repent[14] from evil because of the pain it eventually causes the sinner:

> "Therefore having overlooked the times of ignorance, God is now declaring to men that all everywhere should repent, because He has fixed a day in which He will judge the world in righteousness through a Man whom He has appointed, having furnished proof to all men by raising Him from the dead." (Acts 17:30-31; see also Revelation 16:19)

As previously discussed, this is known as "the fear of the Lord" and its quintessence is to "hate evil" because of the pain it brings (Proverbs 8:13). Since evil is sin, and sin is "the transgression of the Law" (1 John 3:4, KJV), those who walk in observance of God's Laws will be kept from evil:

> "The fear of the Lord tendeth to life: and he that hath it shall abide satisfied; he shall not be visited with evil." (Proverbs 19:23, KJV)

This means that Jabez' prayer for God to keep him from evil was actually a request to keep him obedient to the commandments, because then evil and all its pain could not come upon him.

The Prophet's Message

This is the message God has sent through all His prophets. Those who want to be delivered from evil simply need to turn away from transgressing God's Laws and start obeying them:

> "Yet the LORD warned Israel and Judah, through all His prophets and every seer, saying, 'Turn from your evil ways and keep My commandments, My statutes according to all the law which I commanded your fathers, and which I sent to you through My servants the prophets.'" (2 Kings 17:13)

King and Prophet David understood that the only way to prevent evil from manifesting in his life was to keep God's word:

> "I have restrained my feet from every evil way, that I may keep Thy word."
> (Psalm 119:101)

In His prophetic office, Yeshua asked the Father to keep us from evil by sanctifying us in the Word:

> "I pray not that thou shouldest take them out of the world, but that thou shouldest keep them from the evil. They are not of the world,

even as I am not of the world. Sanctify them through thy truth: thy word is truth." (John 17:15-17, KJV)

God is clearly saying that, when we allow Him to write His laws upon our hearts and remain obedient to them, He keeps us from evil.

Common Hebraic Prayer

This portion of Jabez' petition was part of the standard outline for Hebraic prayer mentioned earlier. Yeshua includes this same appeal in His teaching outline of the Lord's Prayer:

"And lead us not into temptation but deliver us from evil." (Matthew 6:13, KJV)

He is instructing us on how to ask the Lord for strength in resisting the temptation to break His commandments. This is the only way we can escape evil in our lives and become holy vessels for His dwelling.

King David offered up this same request when he prayed:

"Search me, O God, and know my heart: try me, and know my thoughts: and see if there be any wicked way in me, and lead me in the way everlasting." (Psalm 139:23-24, KJV)

The expression "wicked way" is also rendered "way of pain" or "grief" as it was in the prayer of Jabez (Isaiah 14:3; 1 Chronicles 4:9).[15]

The Septuagint and the Vulgate both translate it the "way of iniquity," and the Syriac records it the "way of falsehood."[16]

The root meaning is properly translated an "image" or an "idol" (Isaiah 48:5). Gesenius (Lexicon) terms it "idol-worship." DeWette interprets it as the "way of idols," and Rosenmuller authenticates it to be the "way of an idol."[17]

Simply put, the petition to be kept from evil is a standard Hebraic request for God to search the petitioner's heart for any form of idolatry or defection from the Word. The goal is to uncover any sin so that the individual can turn from it and walk in the "everlasting way" of God's Torah.

This is what Yeshua was referring to when He said, "I know that [God's] commandment is life everlasting" (John 12:50, KJV). It is also what Peter was suggesting when he said:

> "For all flesh is like grass, and all its glory like the flower of grass. The grass withers, and the flower falls off, but the word of the Lord abides forever." (1 Peter 1:24-25)

We know that Peter was referring to the everlasting ways of Torah, because he was quoting from Isaiah 40:8 which is a direct reference to the everlasting laws and commandments of God.

Watch How You Pray

If you earnestly pray for God to "keep or deliver you from evil," watch out, because He is going to expose the idolatry that is in your heart and life. All of us have wickedness in our hearts that we don't even know is there:

> "The heart is deceitful above all things, and desperately wicked: who can know it?"
> (Jeremiah 17:9, KJV)

The primary way that God reveals wickedness in our heart is through a working combination of the Word and the Spirit. First, God reveals sin through the light of Torah. Next, the Holy Spirit convicts us in our hearts and then empowers us to turn from it. Other times the Holy Spirit convicts us first and later, as we study Scriptures, He confirms it through the word.

Sometimes, God reveals wickedness by allowing it to manifest in our lives. Unfortunately, most believers don't realize this when it happens. They attribute the problems that result from their evil ways to the devil, their neighbor, or God Himself. This is typical of man's blame-shifting spirit which goes all the way back to the Garden of Eden:

> And the man said, "The woman whom Thou gavest to be with me, she gave me from the tree, and I ate." (Genesis 3:12)

We have a saying in our ministry that if wickedness (evil/sin/idolatry, etc.) manifests in our lives, it simply means that it is still there. We use the Laws of God to expose it, the blood of Yeshua to forgive it, and the Spirit of God to empower us to turn away from it by keeping His Torah.

Essentially, this is what Jabez prayed for when he asked God to keep him from evil. Hence, Jabez' willingness to repent from any idolatry that God revealed in his heart was the key to the Lord granting him the rest of his prayer.

SIX

SEARCH MY HEART LORD

*"I, the LORD, search the heart, I test the mind,
even to give to each man according to his ways, according to the results of his deeds."*
(Jeremiah 17:10)

HOW MANY OF US are really ready to let the
Lord search our heart and test our mind? Not
many I'm sure. Could the reason be because of all
the idols that He would expose; idols that we are not
yet ready to give up?

Idolatry comprehends the sum of all that is evil. It
comes in many different forms, but it starts whenever we break God's commandments. To break God's
laws is to say that we are equal with God; therefore,
we do not have to submit to Him. At that point, we
become a god unto ourselves, and the idol is the thing
that we are willing to break God's commandments in
order to obtain.

This is exactly what Satan did when he declared,
"I will be like (equal to) the Most High" (Isaiah
14:14, KJV). Then he convinced Adam and Eve that,
if they wanted to "be like God," all they had to do

was break His commandment not to eat of the tree of the knowledge of good and evil (Genesis 3:5).

Consequently, when they transgressed the commandment, they declared themselves to be equal with Yahweh, and the lust for material possessions became mankind's chief idol in the world down to this very day (1 John 2:15-17). This is why the love of money is a root of all evil (1 Timothy 6:10).

Forms of Idolatry

Idolatry comes in numerous shapes and sizes. The most blatant form of idolatry is the worship of a graven image that represents the likeness of another god. Since "God is spirit, and those who worship Him must worship in spirit and truth" (John 4:24), there is no way to make an image of His likeness.

Worshipping the Lord "in spirit and truth" means that we worship God in the power of His Spirit and obedience to the truth of His Word. Both of which are invisible. Consequently, the purpose behind the second commandment is to set the worship of Yahweh apart from all other gods. In other words, the lack of a physical image requires true and unadulterated faith to venerate Him.

Unfortunately, the worship of graven images is

rampant throughout the different religions of the world. It is even practiced in some Christian denominations, where it takes on the form of bowing and praying to statues and altars erected to the dead. One so-called Christian denomination even took the second commandment not to make or worship graven images and rewrote it in such a way that they could. Even though this type of idolatry is easy to spot, many are still seduced by it because idolatry reigns in their hearts.

Another dangerous type of idolatry is the kind that does not appear as a graven image, but it is. I'm talking about any material possession that comes between us and God. This includes automobiles, boats, airplanes, homes, businesses, etc; any tangible possession that would draw our affections away from loving and obeying God.

The next level of idolatry worship is "creation worship" where man puts himself, the animal kingdom, and "mother earth" as a whole on the same level as Yahweh. This is ancient Babylonian pantheism which worships an all-powerful, life-giving, "god force" that they believe comes from the earth itself. This is the worship of a false god that the Lord commands us not to get involved in. To partake of this evil, or even to approve of those who do, promises to bring pain and grief back upon us (Romans 1:21-32).

Then, there is the worship of vice which occurs when various elements of the creation become a god over us. For example, man was given authority over the earth, but when he comes under subjugation to tobacco, a weed from the earth becomes ruler (god) over him. In the same manner, a person who lusts after alcohol allows grain from the earth to become his/her god.

There are also activity idols like sports, hobbies, entertainment, career, etc. that take our focus off of loving and obeying the Lord. For example, if we regularly schedule our fishing, golfing, or other activities during the time when it is customary to attend church, that activity has become an idol. Or if we are in anyway compelled to participate in these activities to the point where it severs our relationship with God or obedience to His Word, then we are in effect serving other gods.

Christian Idols

The most seductive and dangerous idols in the church have a Christian face on them. For example, if the work of the ministry becomes our first love rather that the Lord, than the ministry has become an idol. This is something that Yeshua actually says will be prevalent in the church of the last days, and He commands us to repent of it (Revelation 2:1-5).

Legitimate teachings and movements of God can also become idols if we are not careful. For example, when full immersion water baptism was restored to the church, some falsely taught that a person had to be water baptized in order to be saved. Consequently, water baptism became another god, because it was put on the same level as the blood of Messiah Yeshua.

When God restored the baptism of the Holy Spirit with the evidence of speaking in tongues, many began to chase after the gift of tongues more than they sought God. Like water baptism, many falsely taught that a person had to speak in tongues in order to be saved. Again, this raised a gift of the Holy Spirit to the same level as the blood of God, and it became a religious idol that some groups have built entire denominations around.

I know from first-hand experience that the pre-tribulation rapture is one of the biggest idols in church today. I got saved in 1980 because of my faith in the blood of Yeshua, but my goal was not to serve God; it was to get the heck out of here before things got too bad. I constantly looked to the rapture for my deliverance instead of Yeshua. Then one day, God revealed that I had allowed the pre-tribulation rapture to become another god in my life, which is the case for many in the church today.

The same thing happened with the prophetic movement. When prophets began to rise up and train believers how to flow in the gift of prophecy, many sought to become prophets and/or prophesy more than they sought the Lord. Although we are supposed to desire spiritual gifts, especially that we may prophesy (1 Corinthians 14:1), we are not to desire the gifts more than we do God.

Some of the faith-prosperity message also turned into an idol when ministers started teaching that Christians should have faith in their faith. The only thing that we are to have faith in is God and the truth of His word (Mark 11:22; 2 Thessalonians 2:13). When we have faith in God, we walk according to His commandments and it brings His will for our lives into being. Having faith in our faith instead of God is a form of idolatry that endeavors to make our faith equal to the power and will of God.

The prosperity side of the message was also over-emphasized to the point that it defaulted into a religious get-rich-quick scheme. Rather than giving offerings out of love and obedience to God, many were giving them as a means of coercing God into prospering them, while totally forsaking His commandments in other areas of their lives.

This same thing happened to ancient Israel when they began chasing a perverted idea of prosperity and career-calling. They ended up worshipping two false god's named Fortune and Destiny that brought political and economic destruction:

> "But you who forsake the LORD, who forget My holy mountain, who set a table for Fortune, and who fill cups with mixed wine for Destiny, I will destine you for the sword, and all of you shall bow down to the slaughter." (Isaiah 65:11-12)

This same destruction (war and economic collapse) is currently being released on the entire world system. If we are breaking God's financial laws, we will not escape this destruction no matter how many times a day we pray the prayer of Jabez (Isaiah 65:13-14). We must repent and return to God's laws of prosperity, which includes much more than just sowing "seed-faith" offerings into another man's ministry.

When we commit to return to God's ways, He promises to teach us how to profit according to His commandments (Isaiah 48:17-19). As I clearly explained in my book, *Money & Wealth in the New Millennium*, obedience to God's whole word is the primary thing that releases His blessing and financial prosperity in our lives.

The Prayer Idol

Prayer is one of the most important elements for leading a successful life in the kingdom of God. It is that vital link between us and the Lord, where we receive His strength, direction, provision, and prophetic insight. Prayer opens the life-line between heaven and earth that brings the refreshing wind of God's Spirit.

Unfortunately, prayer has also become an idol for many in the church today. Countless self-proclaimed "prayer warriors" have created the "office of intercessor" that rivals the five-fold offices of apostles, prophets, evangelists, pastors and teachers (Ephesians 4:11). Many have come to idolize this unscriptural office and are currently battling for governmental authority in the church, which shows evidence that Jezebel is in the house.

Intercessory prayer groups have actually become a popular place for Jezebels to hang out and manifest whenever they get a chance. They declared themselves "prophetic intercessors," and endeavor to lead God's bondservant into different forms of idolatry.

As an apostle friend of mine calls it "prophetic divination," because it looks prophetic, but they are divining (calling up) things that are not of God in the name of prayer. If given a position of authority, they will manipulate, intimidate, and attempt to channel the church or the ministry into a form of charismatic witchcraft, that produces destruction in the lives of all involved (Revelation 2:18-29).

There have been a myriad of books written on prayer recently. Some are driven by repetitive formulas that simply turn prayer into a work of the flesh. As I stated in the introduction, God will not answer our prayer just because we pray it three or four or even 1,000 times in a day. When we do this, we are putting our trust in the prayer instead of God, and it becomes an idol.

The unfortunate truth in all of this is that man has an inherent desire to worship something other than the Spirit of the living God. Consequently, everything that is designed to draw us closer to the worship of God has the potential of becoming the object of our worship. When this happens, we end up worshipping those things instead of the Lord and our lives become filled with idolatry. Tragically, this is exactly what has happened to the prayer of Jabez.

Pray and Obey

There are also numerous books and teachings that are well balanced in revealing God's heart concerning prayer. Others explain why and how to pray, but none of them really addresses the issue of obedience as the primary force behind getting our prayers answered.

When we commit to obeying God in all things, it means our heart belongs to Him. If not, it belongs to the enemy. Thus the saying, "If Satan have half the heart, he will have all: if the Lord have but half offered to Him, He will have none."

Yeshua not only came to earth to die for the forgiveness of our sins, but to demonstrate that, when someone loves the Lord with all their heart, it results in their submission to His commandments. Yeshua pointed to His own life as the model for us when He said:

> "If you keep My commandments, you will abide in My love; just as I have kept My Father's commandments, and abide in His love." (John 15:10-11)

The more we abide in God's love, the more we learn to trust the Holy Spirit to live Messiah's life through us. This allows us to yield to His laws without them becoming a burden to us, which is what the Apostle John was referring to when he said:

> "For this is the love of God, that we keep His commandments; and His commandments are not burdensome." (1 John 5:3)

In all of this, I believe God is clearly saying that, if we will return to worship Him in loving obedience to the ancient paths of His Torah, He will give us rest for our souls (Jeremiah 6:16) and answers to our prayers:

> "…whatever we ask we receive from Him, because we keep His commandments and do the things that are pleasing in His sight." (1 John 3:22)

Like Jabez, our love toward God and obedience to His commandments are the real keys that will move God "to grant us that which we request."

ENDNOTES

1   Bruce Wilkinson, The Prayer of Jabez, p 86.

2   "Torah" is defined as: "teaching, direction, instruction (human or divine); the body of prophetic teaching; instruction in the Messianic age; the body of priestly direction or instruction; the body of legal directives." (BibleSoft's online Brown Driver & Briggs Hebrew Lexicon, © 1993, Woodside Bible Fellowship, Ontario, Canada. Licensed from the Institute for Creation Research.)

3   Jamieson, Fausset, and Brown Commentary, Electronic Database, © 1997 by Biblesoft.

4   Ibid

5   Adam Clarke's Commentary, Electronic Database, © 1996 by Biblesoft.

6   Whenever Jesus or the apostles used the terms "word of God", "Scripture", or "It is written," please remember that the New Testament apostolic writings had not been written yet. Consequently, they were referring to the Law (Torah), the prophets (Neviiem), and the writings (Ketivim) of the Tanakh, a.k.a the Old Testament.

7   NT word #3306 from New Exhaustive Strong's Numbers and Concordance with Expanded

Greek-Hebrew Dictionary, © 1994, Biblesoft and International Bible Translators, Inc.; see also Thayer's Greek Lexicon, Electronic Database, © 2000.

8   Ibid, Thayer's Greek Lexicon, Electronic Database, © 2000.

9   OT word #3427 from Biblesoft's New Exhaustive Strong's Numbers and Concordance with Expanded Greek-Hebrew Dictionary, © 1994, Biblesoft and International Bible Translators, Inc. Also see The Online Bible Thayer's Greek Lexicon and Brown Driver & Briggs Hebrew Lexicon, © 1193, Woodside Bible Fellowship, Ontario, Canada. Licensed from the Institute for Creation Research. KJV – (make to) abide (~ing), continue, (cause to, make to) dwell (~ing), ease-eself, endure, establish, X fail, habitation, haunt, (make to) inhabit (~ant), make to keep [house], lurking, X marry (~ing), (bring again to) place, remain, return, seat, set (~tle), (down~) sit (~down, still, ~ting down, ~ting [place] ~uate), take, tarry.

10 If it was not possible for someone to attend one of the feasts in Jerusalem, because of a valid circumstance, they were excused from going. This is why it says that Paul was hurrying to be in

Jerusalem "if possible" on the day of Pentecost (Acts 20:16). The believer simply kept the feast wherever he was at the time, just like Paul did at Ephesus (1 Corinthians 16:8).

11 Vine's Expository Dictionary of Biblical Words, © 1985, Thomas Nelson Publishers, BibleSoft program.

12 1 Kings 7:35; 1 Kings 10:19, Vine's Expository Dictionary of Biblical Words, © 1985, Thomas Nelson Publishers, Biblesoft Program.

13 Hebrew word for "grieve" is the OT word #6087 "atsab" (aw-tsab'); a primitive root; properly, to carve, i.e. fabricate or fashion; hence (in a bad sense) to worry, pain or anger: KJV – displeased, grieve, hurt, make, be sorry, vex, worship, wrest. From Biblesoft's New Exhaustive Strong's Numbers and Concordance with Expanded Greek-Hebrew Dictionary, © 1994, Biblesoft and International Bible Translators, Inc.

14 Repent is the Hebrew word "Teshuvah" and it literally means to turn around 180° from walking in the ways of sin and start walking in the ways of God.

15 Barnes' Notes, Electronic Database, © 1997 by Biblesoft.

16 Ibid

17 Ibid

You may also like to read...

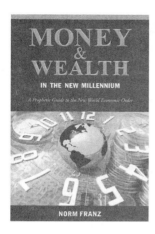

Money and Wealth in the New Millennium

A Prophetic Guide to the New World Economic Order

By Norm Franz
US$19.95, 308 pages
ISBN 0-9710863-0-3

This book is an easy-to-read biblical expose about the global economic problems of the last days and how you can effectively overcome the great end time financial shaking.

"You must read this book if you want to understand what's going on in our economy and what will happen in the future."

- SID ROTH OF MESSIANIC VISION

"I would recommend this book to everyone. There is information in it that I guarantee is worth the price to open its cover."

- KEVIN DEMERITT, PRESIDENT, LEAR FINANCIAL, INC.

Order this book by:
- **Toll free phone number: 800-247-6553**
- **Website:**
  www.moneyandwealthinthenewmillennium.com
- **Visiting your Local Book Store**